Where Is That Tie?

One Tuesday in June, Uncle Mooney was hunting
for his blue tie. First, he tried the closet, but the tie
wasn't there. Then he tried his dresser, but the tie
wasn't there. He even tried underneath the bed, but
the blue tie was still missing.

3

This was a huge problem for Uncle Mooney. The tie was a gift from his nephew, Mike. Every Tuesday afternoon, Mike came over to see the game on TV. Uncle Mooney wore the blue tie. It was good luck.

The Blue Tie

A Division of The McGraw·Hill Companies

Columbus, Ohio

www.sra4kids.com

SRA/McGraw-Hill

A Division of The **McGraw·Hill** *Companies*

Send all inquiries to:
SRA/McGraw-Hill
8787 Orion Place
Columbus, OH 43240-4027

ISBN 0-07-569961-3
5 6 7 8 9 DBH 05

"Hmmm. Last week I spilled root beer on the tie. Maybe Mike took it to be cleaned," said Uncle Mooney to himself. "Mike likes to do nice things like that."

"I know," said Uncle Mooney, "I'll ask Mike's sister, Sue. Maybe she knows. I just hope that Sue picks up the phone. I'd rather not tell Mike that I lost the lucky tie just yet."

Uncle Mooney phoned Mike's house. Sue picked up right away.

"Whew!" said Uncle Mooney. "I'm glad it's you. Do you know whether Mike took my blue tie to be cleaned?"

"No, he didn't," said Sue. "Mike had to take things to the cleaner for Mom, and he didn't have the blue tie when he went."

"Thanks, Sue," said Uncle Mooney. "I hope to see you soon," he added.

"It must be here somewhere," Uncle Mooney muttered to himself. He tried every room in his house. He went into the attic and under the roof beams. He glanced inside his huge tuba. He even looked in his new boots. But there was still no lucky blue tie.

Uncle Mooney began to brood. "Where is
that tie?" he asked himself.

He was so tired from his hunt that he
decided to sit for a bit. Soon, he was napping.

Time to Tell the Truth

Late in the afternoon, Uncle Mooney woke up.

"Oh, no!" he said. "Mike will be here soon. It is too late to do anything about it. I will just have to tell him that I lost the lucky tie."

Uncle Mooney was not in a good mood. He
didn't like to hurt Mike's feelings. When Mike
knocked, Uncle Mooney gloomily opened the
door.

"I'm sorry I'm late," said Mike. "We had
better hurry. The game will be on soon."

Mike went into the living room and turned on the TV. Uncle Mooney went to the kitchen and fixed a tray of snack foods.

"Hurry up, Uncle Mooney. You are going to miss the first pitch," yelled Mike.

There was nothing left to do. Uncle Mooney simply had to tell Mike the bad news. He went to the living room and placed the tray of food on the table.

"Wait!" said Mike. "Uncle Mooney, where's the blue tie? We can't see a game without the lucky blue tie."

Uncle Mooney's face got red and hot. "Well,"
he said to Mike as he unbuttoned his sweater,
"you see. . . I . . . um. . . ."

"There it is!" said Mike. "I knew you wouldn't forget!"

When Uncle Mooney looked, he saw that the blue tie was right there on his neck. He looked back up at Mike and smiled.

"Here," he said, handing Mike the tray, "have a root beer and a few macaroons."